Original title:
Trailing Vines of Thought

Copyright © 2025 Creative Arts Management OÜ
All rights reserved.

Author: Vivienne Beaumont
ISBN HARDBACK: 978-1-80581-719-2
ISBN PAPERBACK: 978-1-80581-246-3
ISBN EBOOK: 978-1-80581-719-2

Layers of Thoughtful Growth

In the garden of my mind, so lush and wild,
Ideas pop up like daisies, a fanciful child.
They twirl and they dance, in a goofy parade,
Each thought like a gnome, in its bright, silly shade.

Thoughts tangle like spaghetti, in a bowl full of cheer,
With sauce made of giggles, and a pinch of weird fear.
I chase after dreams with a kite made of hope,
Yet sometimes I trip, on the end of my rope.

Puns sprout like mushrooms, in rains made of jokes,
As laughter erupts from a cup that just pokes.
Each whimsy a layer, a cake made of jest,
With frosting of folly, it's truly the best!

A parade of ideas, each wearing a hat,
They jest and they jive, oh, imagine that!
In this silly old garden, I grow and I laugh,
Finding joy in each thought, like a warm bubble bath.

Petals of Unspooled Thoughts

A daisy danced on a windy whim,
Chasing shadows, on a whimsy limb.
Thoughts spilled out like spilled rotini,
Sauced with laughter, oh so zany!

Butterflies giggled in the grass,
As ants debated, 'Who's got the sass?'
Petals flutter, a curious sight,
Ideas frolic, morning to night.

The Climb of Unseen Dreams

Up the hill, I trot and sway,
Reaching for thoughts that run away.
One jumped high, then hid in a tree,
Shouting, 'Catch me if you can, whee!'

Ladders made of cotton candy,
Dreams whisper softly, oh so dandy.
With each slip, I laugh and squeal,
Bouncing back, it's all surreal!

Serpentine Patterns of Desire

Wiggly worms on a quest for pie,
Dreaming of sugar clouds in the sky.
Twisting thoughts like a curly fry,
Each one giggles, 'Oh my, oh my!'

Desire slinks like a playful cat,
Sneaking dreams—imagine that!
What's next on this winding spree?
A dance with wishes, just wait and see!

Flourish Beneath the Surface

Beneath the pond, fish throw a bash,
They twirl and swirl, oh what a clash!
Thoughts swim deep in the water's shine,
Bubbles tickle, making them whine.

Lilies giggle, 'Let's break the norm!'
While turtles plot their waterborne charm.
They whisper secrets, swap their tales,
In this laughter, the deep prevails!

Whispers of Twisting Tendrils

In the garden of my brain,
Ideas stretch and twist like grain.
One thought tickles, I burst out laughing,
While another gets lost, its path is baffling.

A crooked path I often find,
With giggles wrapped in each vine unwind.
Thoughts play hide and seek, it's absurd,
Chasing shadows, oh how they've stirred!

A silly notion hops along,
Wearing a hat, singing a song.
The bright ideas dance, prance, and twirl,
While some just trip, and take a swirl.

In this green maze of vibrant laughs,
Where reason and nonsense often halves,
I weave my dreams with absurd delight,
And let my mind bloom, oh what a sight!

Echoes in the Garden of Mind

In the corners, thoughts play peek-a-boo,
One pops up, and then there's two.
They giggle between the flowers with glee,
Spilling secrets like honey from a bee.

With daisies of ideas sprouting wide,
I ride the waves of every tide.
One thought jumps high, a leap so grand,
While another flops down – can't understand!

The squirrels of chaos run amok,
Stealing wisdom like empty socks.
They hide them in the roots with flair,
Telling tales of nonsense everywhere.

Amidst this lush and hearty mess,
I ponder, giggle, and confess.
In this garden where my thoughts unwind,
Every giggle echoes, so unconfined!

The Interwoven Path

On the path where thoughts collide,
I trip over giggles, can't abide.
Winding in circles, I lose my way,
Chasing dreams that just love to play.

Ideas cross like tangled strings,
One snickers softly while another sings.
A little thought walks a zigzag dance,
Inviting the bigger ones to take a chance.

A jumbled mess of quips and puns,
Sprouting wisdom that's far from done.
Each turn I make, more laughter blooms,
With sprigs of humor filling empty rooms.

In the maze where nonsense reigns supreme,
I find a chuckle lost in a dream.
The path is wild, but oh, who cares?
With laughter tangled in my hair!

When Dreams Unravel in the Shade

Under the leafy boughs I sit,
Thoughts unravel like a charming knit.
One whispers softly, a tickling tease,
While the others fall down like autumn leaves.

In this tangled rest, dreams affray,
Chasing butterflies that lead astray.
A giggle curls in the afternoon light,
Spinning tales that bubble with delight.

With shadows casting merry doubt,
I untangle whims that dance about.
Knots of fun twist in the air,
In this dreamy whimsy, I lose my care.

As the laughter echoes through the glade,
It's clear my mind is unafraid.
Finding joy in the dappled sun,
When all my dreams just want to run!

Brambles of Unexamined Paths

I wandered through a field so wide,
Where thoughts grew wild, with nowhere to hide.
I tripped on laughter, fell on a pun,
Stumbled through ideas, just having fun.

Each notion sprouted, twisted in knots,
With every turn, I'd forget what I thought.
In the bouquet of whims, I twirled in place,
Dizzy from musings, a comical chase.

A Tangle of Unvoiced Thoughts

My mind's a jungle, a tangle of vines,
Where silence speaks louder than ten thousand signs.
I chat with my socks, they giggle and tease,
As I ponder the puzzle of frozen peas.

Unspooled ideas roll down the track,
Like runaway cars with no thought to backtrack.
Each twist and turn brings a grin to my face,
Even when I forget, I'll still save the space.

Petals on the Breeze of Mind

Thoughts scatter like petals, light as a breeze,
Floating on laughter, they swirl with such ease.
I chased after giggles, a butterfly's wing,
All tangled in nonsense, oh what fun it did bring!

A picnic of ponderings, crumbs on my lap,
My brain's a buffet, a delightful mishap.
With each mental morsel, I take a big bite,
And laugh at the bites that took flight in the night.

Growing Wings in the Maze of Memory

In the garden of memories, I found a surprise,
A chicken with dreams, disguised as a wise.
It flapped its wings and shared silly tales,
Of socks that sent kites on whimsical sails.

I wandered the maze, lost but still grinning,
Each corner a joke, and I kept on spinning.
With laughter as nectar, I danced with delight,
Growing wings in my mind, taking off into night.

Fragments of a Winding Journey

In a maze of tangled dreams,
Sock puppets plot schemes.
They dance with much delight,
Wearing hats far too tight.

Jellybeans float in the air,
One pink and one rare.
They giggle and they bounce,
As jellybeans often pounce.

The map is upside down,
Leading to a clown town.
Where laughter is a must,
And candy turns to dust.

With rubber chickens in tow,
We step lightly, just so.
On this winding path we roam,
Finding our way back home.

The Language of Climbing Shadows

Whispers in the midnight air,
As shadows dance with flair.
A chair just winked at me,
Should I laugh or flee?

Pinecones try to speak,
With voices strangely meek.
They tumble, trip and roll,
And laugh at their own goal.

The moon crochets with gold thread,
Stitching tales of things said.
A flying toaster flaps,
While the world takes some naps.

Ticklish dreams parade around,
On their silly, happy ground.
Join the fun and forget the night,
As shadows giggle in delight.

Branches of the Soul's Curiosity

Curiosity swings high,
Like a kite in the sky.
Chasing squirrels in a race,
Laughing in an empty space.

Branches stretch like child's play,
Cupcakes tossed in dismay.
They wonder if they can fly,
While clouds just float on by.

Noses twitch, and eyes roll,
A fish jumps, taking its toll.
It dreams of jumping high,
Right up into the sky!

With jelly laughter, we sigh,
Chasing twinkling stars nearby.
Each petal holds a fun story,
In nature's quirky glory.

Entwined in a Whispering Breeze

A breeze came twirling fast,
With secrets from the past.
It tickled trees with glee,
And tangled hair with spree.

Dandelions wear tiny hats,
While wiggly worms converse with bats.
The sun throws a confetti cheer,
As laughter drifts so near.

It spoke of frogs in bow ties,
And jellyfish telling lies.
The breeze whirled in surprise,
As balloons began to rise.

We spun in circles of delight,
While shadows danced with light.
With whimsy in the air we run,
Chasing giggles 'til we're done.

Symphony of Enigmatic Thoughts

In a garden of giggles, ideas bloom,
Whimsical whispers escape from the room.
A thought in a hammock swings back and forth,
Tickling the brain as it dances with mirth.

Nonsense blooms like wildflowers bright,
Each petal a puzzle, a curious sight.
Minds juggle questions with playful delight,
While laughter erupts in the soft summer light.

A melody plays, composed in our heads,
Where answers take naps in cozy warm beds.
Chasing down riddles, oh what a keen chase,
Finding the punchline in a serious place.

Through this symphony of tickles and grins,
Joy takes the lead, where confusion begins.
Each chuckle a note in the chorus we weave,
Creating a tune that no one can leave.

Echoing Frames of Reference

Framed in reflections, a mirror goes wild,
Showing my thoughts like a mischief-filled child.
I gaze at the chaos, it winks with a grin,
These thoughts in a riddle, where do I begin?

Oh look, a giraffe in a top hat and coat,
Taking polite tea with a quirky old goat.
The clock says it's now, but it ticks in reverse,
Turning my logic into a fun little verse.

These wacky reflections bounce back and forth,
Navigating humor like ships sailing north.
Dialogue dances like a game of charades,
Where silly ideas get tangled in braids.

Every echo a laugh, a thought to embrace,
Turning the mundane into an odd race.
In frames full of whimsy, we find our own muse,
As giggles rebuff any serious views.

The Growth of Inward Journeys

Down the rabbit hole of quirky ideas,
I trip on my thoughts, and it tickles my fears.
A cactus in boots starts to cha-cha with me,
And suddenly I'm swept in a whimsical spree.

My brain has a garden, oh what a delight,
Where daisies wear glasses, and sparrows recite.
Each thought is a seed that sprouts in a whirl,
Creating a mess like a fascinating swirl.

Logic takes naps as nonsense runs free,
While I skip through the weeds, what's next? Let's see!
I dance with my doubts, we tango and spin,
Laughing at all the absurdity within.

In this journey of whims, who knows where we land?
Maybe a treasure or just more unplanned.
So I'll frolic through thoughts with a smile on my face,
And let the absurd take me to a bright place.

Winding Paths in Silent Soliloquy

In the maze of my mind, I wander and muse,
Where squirrels debate if it's coffee or juice.
Thoughts twist and turn like a playful charade,
Each corner conceals a delightful tirade.

Oh, what's that sound? A giggle escapes,
From flowers in hats and their playful shapes.
The moon wears a smirk, the stars roll their eyes,
As I chase these odd trails beneath starlit skies.

Whispering secrets my thoughts frequently share,
They trip over jokes with a flair for the rare.
A parade of ideas dances by in the night,
With confetti of laughter that sparkles so bright.

And as I wander down these paths so absurd,
Each step is a chuckle, no need for a word.
In silent soliloquy, joy finds its way,
Curving these winding paths where nonsense can play.

Ribbons of Reflective Serenity

In the garden of the mind, ideas play,
They twirl and spin like kids at a ballet.
Thoughts strut around, dressed in bright hues,
Complaining about the morning's news.

A squirrel scampers past with a nut so round,
He stops to ponder what he might have found.
Meanwhile, my brain is stuck in a loop,
Like pasta that's tangled in one big swoop.

The daisies converse with a daffodil,
Sharing secrets they cannot spill.
Whispers of wisdom float in the breeze,
While I try to remember where I left my keys.

So here's to the laughs that ideas can make,
In this wacky world that we proudly shake.
With every giggle, a new thought is born,
In the garden of chaos, we welcome the morn.

Patterns in the Cerebral Canopy

Beneath the leafy thoughts overhead,
Ideas dangle like threads in a shed.
A cockatoo cackles, tweeting away,
While I ponder dinner and what I'll say.

In this forest of curls and whimsical trails,
Logic plays tag, while reason exhales.
A turtle in glasses claims it's a race,
While I'm figuring out how to tie my shoelace.

Raindrops of laughter splash on my head,
Each droplet a memory I've carefully bled.
With squirrels debating the best nut to choose,
I'm just here giggling, can't help but snooze.

So let's dance with the shadows, skip through the light,
In this jungle of humor, everything's bright.
Here in my mind, imagination's the queen,
Where life's all a joke, and I'm just the scene.

Whorls of Wondering Hearts

In a whirlpool of musings, hearts take a spin,
Like a dog chasing tails it can never win.
Thoughts bounce around like popcorn unpopped,
Turning serious moments to giggles that dropped.

Here comes a rabbit, with spectacles on,
He's crafting deep theories till the break of dawn.
With each scribbled thought, he looks quite absurd,
Yet he jumps high in joy, like nobody heard.

Thoughts swirl in circles, dizzying and bright,
While I stand in the corner, a comical sight.
Tangled in laughter, I wave my arms wide,
As ideas collide like a roller-coaster ride.

So here's to the hearts that wonder and roam,
Finding joy in the chaos, feeling right at home.
In this carnival of whimsy, we all play a part,
Laughing aloud with our whimsical hearts.

Intricacies of the Intellectual Garden

In the garden of smarts, weeds pop up in glee,
Telling tall tales as they tickle the knee.
A bumblebee buzzes, wearing a hat,
Debating the virtues of cheese and of rat.

Petunias are pondering about world affairs,
While dandelions spin wild through the air.
Roots intertwine like gossiping friends,
Whispering secrets that never have ends.

A butterfly flutters with wisdom it stole,
From a worm who was reading a self-help scroll.
With each little giggle, new blooms start to rise,
In this quirky retreat, imagination flies.

So let's revel in nonsense, let laughter abound,
For in this odd garden, joy's always found.
With humor as sunlight, we'll grow and we'll sway,
In the intricacies of thought, we'll happily play.

Weaving Whispers of the Soul

In a world where thoughts just prance,
Ideas twirl, they love to dance.
A sock lost here, a hat misplaced,
In my mind's garden, chaos is chased.

A noodle bends, a frown flips fast,
My brain's a circus, not built to last.
With juggling thoughts and pies in the air,
I laugh at the mess, life's a funny affair!

Whispers tickle like leaves in the breeze,
Words slip and slide with relative ease.
A ticklish thought that zigs and zags,
Fleeting moments like cheeky rags.

Through tangled tales, giggles entwine,
As I sip my tea, a real good sign.
Riding the waves of whimsical calls,
With editing pens and laughter for all.

Whims of the Wandering Spirit

Skipping stones on puddled plans,
The mind does cartwheels, yes, it can!
Chasing birds and dodging rain,
This joyful jest is never plain.

A squirrel's dance, a butterfly's fling,
Thoughts bubble up like a quirky spring.
With jests that twinkle, shiny and bright,
The wandering spirit takes flight tonight.

In the realm where giggles roam free,
A tickle of mischief, just let it be!
Cotton candy dreams float in the air,
While I laugh at my thoughts without a care.

Wandering whims with sparkly flair,
Through silly antics, ideas declare.
With laughter the lantern, bright and true,
Every step a jest, just me and you.

Fronds of Faded Memories

A film reel spins of silly tales,
Where laughs once grew, now whimsy pales.
My memory sways like a drunk pogo stick,
Recalling moments that vanish quick.

Jumbled jigsaw, pieces all askew,
I hold tight to the few that stick like glue.
Frogs on bikes in a fishy parade,
Turning like pages, I'm greatly dismayed.

With echoes of chuckles from days of yore,
I stumble on puns through the open door.
Snapshot of laughter, aged like fine cheese,
Where sadness gets lost like leaves in the breeze.

Faded memories lead to hopeful laughs,
As I sift through my past like a wizard's staffs.
In a treasure chest of oddities bold,
Each quirk a story, forever retold.

The Curves of Contemplative Springs

The water bubbles with giggles, it seems,
As thought takes a dive into whimsical dreams.
A rubber duck floats, wearing a grin,
While questions pop up like bubbles from within.

A rollercoaster ride through reasons absurd,
Chasing the punchline, not grasping the word.
The sinewy giggles, the twists and the bends,
Life takes a turn where humor transcends.

With each little splash in the pool of my mind,
Silly perspectives are joyfully blind.
In contemplations, laughter takes its wing,
Bouncing around like it's made for a fling.

Thoughts pirouette and leap through the air,
Making light of the burdens we wear.
So let's flow together on this zany stream,
In curves of amusement, let's just be gleamed.

Blooming in the Silence

In gardens where spaghetti is tossed,
To flowers that claim they've been lost.
The bees hold debates on who's the best,
While daisies sigh, taking a rest.

A cornflower wears sunglasses bright,
Says, "I shine best in the night!"
While tulips throw shade, just for fun,
And giggle when day is finally done.

The daisies dance, a clumsy affair,
With petals that fly through the air.
They whisper of secrets in bloom,
While violets plan a grand costume.

In still of the night, if you listen close,
You'll catch what they say, and then some prose.
For laughter can grow on a whispering breeze,
In gardens alive with giggles and tease.

Murmurs Beneath the Surface

The river chuckles, a playful tease,
Saying, "Oh fish, go dance with the trees!"
With ripples that giggle, a watery cheer,
While frogs hold a concert, quite loud and clear.

Beneath the waves, the catfish conspire,
Plotting to start a deep-sea choir.
And turtles, with hats, drum on their shells,
While minnows weave tales no one quite tells.

The reeds sway in rhythm, quite unlike before,
Whispering of legends where sea tales galore.
A crab takes a bow, with claws in full form,
In this underwater, humorous norm.

So dive in the ripples, hear all that's said,
With laughter afloat and wonders to tread.
For beneath the surface, a party in play,
Where water's alive in the quirkiest way.

Roots of Hidden Insight

Beneath our feet, where secrets lie,
The roots have gossip, oh my, oh my!
They dig underground, with stories to tell,
Of acorns and nuts, and mischief as well.

The radish holds court, with a bemused glance,
Saying, "I've seen potatoes try to dance!"
While carrots throw shade to turnip's new dress,
Claiming that greens just can't handle the stress.

Under the soil, there's laughter and cheer,
As worms discuss dreams of growing up here.
With broccoli crowned in an underground show,
The roots sing a tune only plants seem to know.

So next time you ponder beneath the green,
Remember the laughter, the unseen machine.
For life's hidden wisdom rests not on the hill,
But roots in the ground, gathering laughter still.

Lattice of Longing

A web of wishes, all tangled and spun,
The dreams of the old, of the young, and the fun.
With stars that play hopscotch across the bright skies,
And giggles that echo, where whimsy first lies.

The shadows hold parties, where spirits entwine,
With lanterns of laughter and jests that align.
A moonbeam tips hats to the clouds as they roll,
And dreams play their charades, that's the goal.

From dusk until dawn, the wishes flit fast,
A lattice of humor, a spell that can't last.
With jokes carved in starlight, and puns in the breeze,
While nostalgia waltzes with whimsical ease.

So capture these moments, keep them in mind,
For laughter's like gold, the rarest of finds.
In every small tangle, a chuckle we find,
A lattice of longing, silly and kind.

Cascading Consciousness

Thoughts tumble down like a playful stream,
Chasing ideas like a daydream team.
I'm lost in laughter, my mind takes flight,
Juggling giggles in the soft twilight.

Every thought a pebble, each splash a grin,
I dive into nonsense, let the fun begin.
Waves of whimsy surge in my head,
Riding the currents of what I said.

A kooky parade of quirky muse,
Dancing with jesters, I can't refuse.
The echoes of laughter ripple and roll,
Painting a canvas, tickling the soul.

So let's tumble down this wild highway,
Where silly ideas come out to play.
In this cascading dream, I sip my tea,
And dip into laughter, just being me.

The Garden of Echoing Silence

In a garden where thoughts bloom like vines,
Whispers of echoes spin tangled lines.
I chuckle at shadows that dance on the lawn,
Sipping on silence from dusk until dawn.

Beneath bright sun like an echoing giggle,
Ideas sprout up and then do the wiggle.
I twirl with the daisies in whimsical glee,
As bees buzz their secrets, just me and the trees.

Quietly loud, this garden's a feast,
Where thoughts grow so wild, I'm just a beast.
Puns blend with petals, all nature's wit,
In the echo of silence, I'm finally fit.

A harvest of humor, ripe for the pick,
With every new whim, I'm ready to tick.
So plant me a joke, or two or three,
In this glorious garden, wild and free.

Whispers of Cognitive Flora

Flora of thought whispering seeds of jest,
Giggling daisies put my mind to the test.
Each bloom's a riddle, a pun on the ground,
In this mental meadow, silliness found.

Petals of laughter take flight on a breeze,
Fields of confusion bring me to my knees.
Roots of my musings twist like a pretzel,
Tangled recollections refuse to settle.

In this forest of giggles, I stop and stare,
A squirrel with a bowtie, what a sight rare!
Thoughts bouncing around like a ball in a game,
Planting the seeds of my inner acclaim.

Call it a jungle, this wild mental spree,
Where funny ideas abound, just like me.
In whispers of flora, my mind dances free,
Exploring the wonders of what can't be.

Stems of Inner Harmony

In the garden of thoughts where silliness grows,
Stems of my ideas stretch out like prose.
I'm giggling at clouds, they're head in the air,
While flowers in bowties start a zany affair.

Harmony dances on a jumpy breeze,
Twirling with fancies and chuckling trees.
One moment I'm serious, the next, I trip,
On roots of my musings, I take a small sip.

Armed with my laughter, I'm ready to sing,
To the beat of my thoughts, oh, what joy they bring!
Inner delight like the sunshine above,
Sprouting a chorus of whimsical love.

With every small giggle, the world shines bright,
As stems intertwine through the canvas of light.
So let's frolic and play in this blissful design,
And dance with our thoughts like a vintage wine.

Tangles of Time and Memory

In the attic, boxes stacked high,
Old photos whisper, oh my!
Each face a puzzle, lost in space,
Like socks unmatched, what a race!

Dust bunnies dance, having a ball,
While my brain tries to recall,
Was that a cousin or a friend?
Oh no, where does this story end?

Time's a jester, tricks up its sleeve,
Making us laugh, but we can't believe,
That memories tangled like yarn on the floor,
We untwist them, then drop them once more!

So here's to the past, we giggle and sigh,
With every lost thought, we give it a try,
A treasure hunt of the mind we embrace,
In this goofy, chaotic memory chase!

Echoes of Spiraling Serenity

On a lazy chair, I sit and spin,
Thoughts like Frisbees, where to begin?
Should I ponder the cat or the moon?
Or just sing a silly, off-key tune?

In spirals they twirl, like dervishes bold,
Ideas are noodles, too slippery to hold,
One moment I'm deep in the meaning of life,
The next, I'm just thinking 'bout butter and rye!

Serenity laughs, a snicker so sweet,
As I chase visions of a dancing beet,
Intentions may wobble like jelly on toast,
But who can resist the whims of a ghost?

So let's embrace the chaos of cheer,
With echoes that tingle, oh so near,
For laughter rings true in the fog of the mind,
And serenity's echoes are one of a kind!

The Canopy of Infinite Paths

Under the trees, my thoughts run wild,
Like children playing, oh so mild,
Which way to go? A fork in the wood,
Follow the squirrels? It can't be that good!

Paths twist and turn, like a pretzel so grand,
Every choice leads to a place unplanned,
Should I chat with the fox or dance with a hare?
Oh wait, where's my map? I'm trapped in despair!

Infinite journeys on this green tapestry,
Each step unfolding a comical spree,
A laugh at the stumbling, a giggle at fate,
Who knew lost in nature could be so great?

So come grab your boots, let's frolic and roam,
In this canopy of paths, we'll find our way home,
With every mishap, we'll chuckle and cheer,
For the joy of the journey is perfectly clear!

Threads of Nature's Wisdom

In the garden of dreams, wisdom grows,
With a sprinkle of laugh, and a pinch of prose,
Rabbits debate under whispering trees,
While I ponder a cupcake, oh how it appease!

Nature's threads weave a tapestry bright,
With every flower, they dance in delight,
A bee buzzes by with a comical grin,
Polling for nectar, where do I begin?

Squirrels take notes, as acorns fall down,
What wisdom they share, worthy of a crown,
"Don't take life too seriously," they seem to say,
"For every silly moment should brighten your day!"

So let's tip our hats to the world all around,
Embrace the strange wisdom that's silly and sound,
For in every mess-up, a lesson is found,
In threads of laughter, joy does abound!

Tendrils of Memory's Embrace

A noodle of thought, it twists and bends,
Like spaghetti left out, it never ends.
These memories cling, like socks in the wash,
What is this kaleidoscope, a silly nosh?

They linger and dance, like gum on the shoe,
Recollections of moments, all silly and blue.
A birthday cake candle, I forgot to blow,
Now it's a saga, how did I not know?

Each thought's a balloon, some float up so high,
While others just pop, oh me, oh my!
I chase after them, but they giggle and flee,
Just like cats with a laser, oh woe is me!

In corners they lurk, these jests of the mind,
Whispering secrets that I've left behind.
I chase them like cows in a pasture so wide,
These tendrils of memory with nowhere to hide.

Blossoms of Contemplation

A ponder blooms bright, like daisies in spring,
But trip on a thought, oh, what a wild fling!
Each petal a query, all flutter and sway,
Am I thinking too much, or just lost in the fray?

What if cows could talk, or bananas could sing?
That's a thought blossom I'd sure like to bring!
I'll plant it in soil, and watered with glee,
Watch it sprout giggles, come grow wild with me!

These blooms of absurdity smell fresh like a fume,
They tickle my brain, and pop like a boom!
Each flower a jest, growing taller with height,
I'm musing on nonsense, oh what a delight!

In gardens of pondering, I wander around,
Where laughter sprouts up from whimsical ground.
So come share the blooms, let's skip and let's prance,
In this patch of strange thoughts, let's twirl and dance!

The Labyrinth of Inner Growth

In the maze of my mind, I chase and I dart,
Got lost in the cornfield, but it's just a start.
The walls are made of giggles, the floors made of cheese,
One wrong turn, and I'm down on my knees!

Each corner I turn, there's a joke that I find,
A riddle left hanging, just dangling behind.
My wisdom's a puzzle, like socks in a load,
Somehow I'm thinking of frogs on the road!

I'm stuck in this tangle, lost in my schemes,
Where pathways are lined with my silly dreams.
With each step I take, my laughter may grow,
In this inner turmoil, there's joy in the flow!

I wander through shadows of all that I've learned,
What's real and what's not, is a line I've not turned.
But with every twist, there's a chuckle, a grin,
In this labyrinth of learning, I'm ready to win!

Spirals of Uncharted Ideas

I'm riding on thoughts, on a merry-go-round,
Spinning so fast, I've lost solid ground.
Do cows wear pajamas? I ponder this still,
With each twirl I take, I'm just feeding the thrill!

Ideas like balloons are floating up high,
Some drift into clouds, while others just cry.
I grab at the colors, a rainbow of whim,
Why is the sky purple? Oh, where've I been?

Each concept an octopus, flailing about,
I chase down the tentacles, wriggling in doubt.
What if my toaster could toast toast that could sing?
Then breakfast would rock, oh, what joy it would bring!

So come join this dance on the spirals of thought,
Let's giggle at nonsense, and all that we've sought.
For in every twirl, there's a spark in our brains,
In these uncharted ideas, fun forever remains!

Entangled in Inner Landscapes

In the garden of my mind, I stroll,
Where thoughts like weeds take a playful roll.
With fronds that twist and giggle so bright,
They dance 'round the memories, what a delight!

A thought jumps high, a tangle of joy,
Eluding the logic every girl and boy.
I chase after laughter, I trip on a rhyme,
Who knew pondering could be such a climb?

With roots that grip my tangled brain,
These silly ideas drive me quite insane.
Yet with every chuckle, I'm light as a leaf,
For in this chaos, I find my relief!

So let's twirl in this botanical fray,
Where thoughts just frolic, come out and play.
Each vine a giggle, each leaf a cheer,
In this garden of whims, I've no fear!

Veins of Intuitive Wisdom

In the town of my brain, ideas parade,
With insights like puppies, they leap and they wade.
Some are pure genius, others just fluff,
But isn't it funny? I can't get enough!

Wisdom flows like syrup, thick but so sweet,
You slip on a thought, then land on your feet.
Laughing at fumbles that tumble along,
It's in the quirks that I find my song!

Ideas wriggle like worms on a spree,
Who knew a brainstorm could feel so carefree?
With intuitive giggles that rattle my core,
You'd think in this wisdom there's always a score!

So gather 'round friends, let's giggle and muse,
In the veins of insight, there's no time to lose!
Each chuckle contagious, we'll ride this wild tide,
With the zany of thinking, we'll laugh, we'll collide!

The Ferns of Contemplative Space

In the corner of quiet, thoughts bubble and brim,
While ferns on the windowsill whisper and grin.
They sway to the rhythm of what's next to come,
Each one a riddle, quite unintentionally dumb!

As I ponder and wander through ideas galore,
The ferns break the silence with giggles and snore.
They tease out my worries, they tickle my brain,
In this lush little haven, there's no need for pain!

Elaborate thoughts weave a tapestry dense,
With knots that can't unravel, quite counter-intense.
Yet laughter erupts like a pop in the air,
These ferns are my buddies; they simply don't care!

So let's sit in this garden and savor the zest,
While thoughts do the cha-cha, and laughter's the guest.
With each sway and twist, I'll bet you agree,
This contemplative space is where hearts can be free!

Undulating Currents of Reflection

Thoughts undulate like waves in the sea,
Bobbing and weaving, they giggle with glee.
Reflections that shimmer like fish in the foam,
Each splash a notion, so strange and so roam!

Ticklish ideas ride the currents of time,
Making silly faces like clowns in a rhyme.
I paddle through puddles of whimsy and jest,
In this ocean of thought, I'm simply a guest!

Wisdom's a flounder that flips with a splash,
Caught in the currents, it's quite a mad dash!
Yet laughter's the anchor, keeping me still,
As I float through these waters, embracing the thrill!

So let's dive deeper into this vast delight,
Where waves of reflection bring giggles by night.
Here in the ocean of silly delight,
I wave to my thoughts, as they frolic in flight!

Embers of Existential Reflection

In the garden of my mind, I find,
A gnome wearing shoes, how unrefined!
He dances with doubts, but they all flee,
While pondering if he should drink his tea.

The sun shines bright on my silly side,
Where thoughts tumble down like a wobbly ride.
Should I bake a cake or just take a nap?
Oh wait, I forgot I was planning a map!

With every flurry of whimsy that spins,
I laugh as my pondering quietly grins.
What if the universe was made of cheese?
Then every moonbeam smells just like a breeze!

So here in this chaos, I take my seat,
On a cloud made of marshmallows, soft and sweet.
With giggles and chuckles my thoughts intertwine,
In this spark of existence where humor will shine.

Sways of Imaginative Growth

A tree in my thoughts sways left and right,
With squirrels in capes causing quite the fright!
They plan grand heists for acorns at night,
While debating if crows are all feathered knights.

Imagining worlds where jellybeans fly,
And rainfalls of chocolate drip from the sky.
Do birds wear sunglasses when sunbathing high?
Oh goodness, my mind's quite the kooky sci-fi!

I wonder if fish can play chess on a whim,
Or if frogs lead parades on a bright golden rim.
Does time stop to laugh when it trips on a limb?
These thoughts dance around like a gleeful hymn!

In fields of odd notions, I dash and I dart,
Collecting bright dreams as I skip and I start.
With each silly story, I paint and create,
The laughter of life is my favorite fate.

Oasis of Ponderous Possibilities

In an oasis where thoughts sip on tea,
A cactus tells jokes, as funny as can be.
Do turtles wear hats when they stroll by the sea?
This very debate makes me giggle with glee!

The clouds play charades while raindrops pretend,
Time twirls with a wink and struggles to bend.
Are there socks for each planet? Oh, what a trend!
If aliens join in, maybe they can lend!

With each little question, the sun starts to grin,
While shadows dance lightly, inviting a spin.
Do all of our worries come from within?
Well, I'll just keep laughing till the day I win!

So, here in my haven, where hilarity blooms,
Laughter resounds, filling all of the rooms.
I sip on my thoughts like a fine cup of cheer,
Creating a world where fun is sincere.

The Architecture of Forgetfulness

In a city of thoughts built on sandy ground,
A baker constructs dreams with giggles unbound.
With cupcakes and lollipops spinning around,
Each layer of laughter in frosting is found.

The blueprints of whimsy are scattered with flair,
While wandering thoughts tangle up in midair.
A raccoon in a top hat claims he's a millionaire,
As squirrels give speeches on fluffy despair!

Do chairs have opinions when no one is home?
And do carpets conspire whenever they roam?
I question the logic as I sit and comb
Through memories lost in the grandest of foam.

In this architecture of giggles and glee,
The past is a canvas, the present is free.
With whimsy as mortar, my walls are a spree,
I'm building a fortress from laughter, you see!

Shadows of Unraveled Sentences

Words dance like shadows, all out of line,
Each phrase trips over, oh what a sign!
Puns lurking hidden, like gremlins in dark,
Echoes of laughter, oh what a lark!

Jumbled reflections in a puddle of prose,
Where humor and nonsense entwine like a rose.
Tickles of giggles where grammar's a mess,
But hey, it's a party, let's all just confess!

Thoughts run in circles, take a wild spin,
Logic sprints off while silliness grins.
Poking fun at the serious game,
We laugh at the shadows that carry our name!

So let's unravel each knot of our minds,
With chuckles and hiccups, the best kind of finds.
For in this wild maze where coherence is shy,
We'll dance through the chaos, you and I!

Spirals of Inner Dialogue

Whispers of chatter swirl 'round in my head,
Debates with a sandwich about what's for bread!
Inner monologues play hide and seek,
While my thoughts throw a rave, oh, how unique!

A rubber chicken jokes with a philosophical cat,
Questions their existence—imagine that!
Who knew deep thinking could be such a hoot?
As the noodle thoughts frolic, all wild and cute!

Round and round they tumble, like leaves in the breeze,
Pondering life over bowls of warm cheese.
In nutty discussions, reason gets lost,
But who needs it anyway? Just accepting the cost!

Chasing the spirals, I find tasty delights,
Each turn brings a giggle, sparks silly flights.
So let's celebrate ramblings, the chaos we share,
In this merry uproar, we find joy everywhere!

Threads of Whimsy and Wonder

Tangled in thoughts that dance and entwine,
A unicorn sneezes—what a great sign!
Laughter erupts from the seams of my mind,
As whimsy and wonder get blissfully blind.

A jester in overalls winks from afar,
With threads of absurdity, he's raising the bar.
Weaves tales of dandelions playing the fool,
In a garden of giggles, oh, isn't this cool?

Kites made of cookies soar high in the sky,
While raccoons in tuxedos collect the pie.
Lost in this fabric of joy, I find peace,
As the threads of my whims never seem to cease!

So join in the laughter, let's spin this delight,
For in threads of whimsy, all wrongs feel quite right.
In the tapestry of chuckles, let's play and conspire,
With each goofy twist setting our hearts on fire!

The Twists of Memory's Path

Once I lost my sock on a journey of thought,
It turned into a monster that never got caught!
With a wiggly snicker, it twisted away,
Leaving trails of confusion that brightened my day.

Paths paved with giggles and moments so strange,
Where nonsense and genius commute and exchange.
I recall riding llamas through walls of blue cheese,
While polka-dot penguins danced light on their knees!

Memory's a riddle with paths that unwind,
Full of quirky surprises that tickle the mind.
Forgotten a message? Oh, what a delight,
When whispers of silly replace the outright!

So let's wander and spin down the memory lane,
Where twists and turns make us giggle again.
With every peculiarity that life brings to view,
We'll toast to the trail of what once seemed askew!

Veils of Reflection

In the garden where secrets tease,
I found my thoughts wrapped in the breeze.
A squirrel sneered, a bird gave a wink,
While I pondered over what to think.

Each leafy whisper had a tale to share,
Of missed opportunities and lost love affairs.
The daisies giggled as I tripped on a root,
Reminding me of my childhood pursuit.

Reflections danced on the pond's placid face,
I laughed at the frog in a princely embrace.
He croaked a joke about jumping too high,
While I plotted ways to fly with the sky.

Yet here I sit with a pen and a snack,
My thoughts like vines, just can't hold back.
With every chuckle and every odd twist,
I wonder if daydreams are too hard to resist.

Nature's Ink on Paper

The meadow's my canvas, wild and free,
With daisies as brushes, they smile at me.
A bumblebee buzzes like it's leading a choir,
While I scribble nonsense and call it desire.

Pine trees stand tall, but they often forget,
How to keep quiet when I place my bet.
With every rustle, a story unfolds,
As if the wind's gossip is all that it holds.

Ants line up, a parade of ambition,
Mapping the world with perfect precision.
Yet here I am, with ink stains galore,
Contemplating if dust had a secret lore.

With clouds as my muses, I aim for the stars,
While grasshopper laughter fills up the jars.
Nature's the script, I'm just here for the ride,
Each moment a chuckle, unplanned and untried.

Greenery of Forgotten Dreams

In a thicket of whims, where strange thoughts cling,
Weeds sing a song like a kooky old king.
They reminisce tales of glory and snack,
While I sip tea from a very odd crack.

Laughter erupts from the roots of a tree,
As I query the sap, what it thinks of me.
It grins with delight, "You're welcome to stay,
Though we all know that the sun steals the day."

Clouds roll in, playing peek-a-boo games,
While grass rolls its eyes at the proclamations of fame.
Each petal has words, though I can't take the hint,
So I scribble my thoughts with a sporadic glint.

Amongst the green hugs, my dreams start to bloom,
Chasing after laughter, I clear out the gloom.
Who knew that nature could be such a clown?
In this jungle of thoughts, I wear no frown.

Shadows Beneath the Canopy

Under the leafy roof where whispers collide,
I found an old shadow who's been here awhile.
It tells silly stories of when it was spry,
And offers a nap, just to give it a try.

The ferns giggle softly, their fronds in a twist,
As a squirrel flips acorns, claiming no tryst.
Each stretch of the vines brings chuckles and glee,
While I chase after thoughts like a child on a spree.

Sunbeams do salsa, they dance on the ground,
While the shadows reply with a flicker and bound.
The chattered old wind carries secrets right by,
As I scratch down the tales 'neath the wandering sky.

So here in the shade, with laughter afloat,
I sip on my worries, like a daydreamy boat.
The world feels so goofy, so light on its feet,
While shadows keep spinning their whimsical beat.

Nectar of Contemplative Blooms

In a garden of giggles, ideas sprout,
Sipping from thoughts, oh what a route!
The bees buzz with laughter, a silly brigade,
They dance on the petals, unafraid.

Above in the branches, a squirrel takes notes,
On acorn philosophies, and nutty quotes.
He scribbles with vigor, in sunbeam's embrace,
While pondering his snack, with style and grace.

The daisies are plotting a boisterous game,
While tulips join in, thinking they're all the same.
A sunflower winks, brings comedic flair,
As petals engage in a dandelion dare.

Yet amidst all the fun, blooms wisdom profound,
In humor's sweet nectar, true knowledge is found.
So join in the laughter, the jests all around,
For in the garden of thought, joy doth abound.

Budding Ideas in Silent Spaces

In a quiet nook, a shadow goes 'pop!',
A bright idea jumps and does a soft flop.
With giggles and chuckles, it starts to unfold,
A tale of mishaps, both silly and bold.

The chairs start to chatter, the table joins in,
As a loaf of bread laughs at the whisking spin.
The butter begins sliding, a slippery act,
In this silent space, laughter's the pact.

A tomato dreams big, it wants to be saucy,
While basil rolls over, calling it bossy.
Together they giggle, a kitchen surprise,
Where muddled ideas burst, and joy multiplies.

Then silence returns, but the smiles remain,
As budding creations whisper in vain.
For even in quiet, the fun finds a way,
To tickle the mind, and lighten the day.

Whispers of Winding Minds

Whispers drift softly like feathers in air,
Thoughts twist and tumble without a care.
Like cats chasing shadows, they frolic and roam,
Creating a labyrinth, a cerebral home.

One thought becomes crooked, then makes a U-turn,
While laughter erupts at the pages they churn.
A hamster on wheels, it speeds up the chase,
In this game of ideas, there's no need for space.

A butterfly grins, it's dappled in thought,
As it flutters through laughter, all lessons are caught.
The moon beams a chuckle, the stars wink with glee,
As whispers of winding minds flow endlessly free.

In this maze of humor, a truth comes to light,
That silliness blesses the shadows of night.
So let's dance through the corridors, merry and spry,
For the winding whispers open a gateway to fly.

Echoes of Entwined Dreams

In the realm of the fanciful, dreams interlace,
With giggles and chuckles, they dance in a race.
A pickle contemplates, "Can I fly in a stew?"
While carrots all laugh at the things they can't do.

The onions are scheming a splashy parade,
With garlic as conductor, making sure they're displayed.
Zucchini joins in, sprouting fanciful tales,
As they echo their dreams through whimsical trails.

Bubbles of laughter float high in the sky,
As radishes aim for the clouds, oh my!
The audience cheers, a spectacle grand,
As echoes of joy sweep across the land.

So gather your thoughts, let them twirl and spin,
In this garden of humor, let the fun begin.
For echoes of entwined dreams shall remind,
That laughter and folly are all intertwined.

Tendrils of Reflection

In a tangle of thoughts, I find my way,
Chasing bubbles that float, come what may.
Lost in the daydreams, I giggle and sway,
Like a cat on a mission, too wild for the fray.

With a wink at the chaos, I dance in the sun,
Counting my giggles, oh what fun!
Questions like balloons, bobbing one by one,
Pop! Went the worries, I'm not quite done!

Thoughts like spaghetti, all twirly and whirly,
I fork them with laughter, it's all kind of swirly.
Each twist is a riddle, quite silly, quite burly,
I'll keep laughing, won't take it all thoroughly.

So here's to the puzzles, the spirals, the plays,
Where nonsense erupts in whimsical ways.
In gardens of giggles, I'll spend all my days,
Twirling my thoughts in a dizzying haze.

Fragments of a Wandering Muse

A little bird whispered my mind's in a haze,
I chased it around for the better part of days.
She sang about socks that dance in strange ways,
And how spaghetti can be the sun's warm rays.

My muse plays hide and seek in the kitchen,
Winking at cookies and cakes she's bewitchin'.
Every plate's a canvas, I'm left here glitchin',
Creating recipes that need… some revision.

Thoughts bloom afresh like weeds in the garden,
One sprouts a question, then two come a-bargain.
"Why do we frown when the trees are so pardon?"
"Because I once sat on one, and it left me harden!"

In the kitchen of ideals, the pots over boil,
As ideas rise up with a laughing recoil.
I gather the fragments, all tattered and spoiled,
Flavored with giggles, these thoughts I embroil.

Cascades of Contemplation

Idea cascades like a waterfall's rush,
Plopping like raindrops in a big squishy mush.
Each splash has a concept, a thought, or a hush,
I dive right in, feeling inspired and flush.

Thoughts tumble like olives in a wild dance,
Rolling alongside all the puns that entrance.
Who knew that the fridge could prompt such a chance?
To ponder the art of a snack in a trance?

From lemons to limes, the flavors collide,
In this banquet of humor, I take a wild ride.
Ideas like confetti, they scatter with pride,
While I spin my thoughts in a goofball stride.

So wade in the river where laughter flows free,
Let giggles and musings be the sparkly spree.
In the whirlpool of whimsy, come join me and see,
How a splash of absurdity can set your mind free!

Labyrinths in the Garden of Ideas

A maze made of chuckles, where thoughts twist and twine,
I wander the pathways, sipping on sunshine.
With a hat made of giggles, my worries decline,
As I dance through the aisles of the dreamer's design.

In one corner, a parrot is juggling some glee,
While in another, a snail sings a jolly decree.
Each path leads to laughter, a tangle, you see,
As I wiggle and wriggle in utter glee.

Ideas sprout like flowers, colors bright and bizarre,
Petals of puns flutter like clouds from afar.
I sip on my musings from a teacup-shaped star,
Dreaming of worlds where no thought's ever marred.

So come join the hunt in this absurdity map,
Where wisdom and whimsy weave snug in a lap.
You'll find in the laughter, there's always a gap,
And the pearls of our folly are the gold that we clap.

Shadows of the Reflective Canopy

In a garden of worries, I trip and I fall,
My queries stretch upwards, they tango with walls.
A squirrel named Fred whispers 'Life's just a jest!'
While pondering pastries, I muse like a pest.

With each fleeting thought, a balloon starts to drift,
It tells me that chips are a wonderful gift.
My brain is a circus, it's tumbling down,
With laughter and giggles, I wear a sly crown.

Beneath leafy arches, my dreams sway like trees,
While ants hold a meeting and debate with the bees.
I wax poetic on colors that shine,
The funny things we ponder, in a day that's divine.

Amidst shadows so playful, my mind takes a spin,
Where thoughts are akin to a jazz violin.
So let's raise a toast to the odd and the strange,
For in this wild maze, it's a delightful change!

The Circuitry of Introspection

Inside my head, a computer's at play,
With wires all tangled, it's leading astray.
A pop-up appears, 'Have you fed your cat?'
I burst into giggles, just where am I at?

My neurons are dancing, like robots in line,
They say 'Don't forget, you left clothes on the line!'
Every thought is a circuit, it whirs and it sparks,
While I summon old memories, like quirky remarks.

Electric conversations, a spark in my brain,
With thoughts racing faster, like cars in the rain.
I'm lost in the system, it's a wild domain,
So bring on the laughter, let joy be my gain!

In this grand computer, where nonsense is king,
The glitches and giggles make my spirit sing.
A network of chuckles, I strive to unwind,
As the circuitry buzzes, I'm blissfully blind!

Reverie in a Canopy of Thought

Under blue canopies of whimsical dreams,
Where thoughts run in circles and burst at the seams.
A turtle named Gary tells jokes at my feet,
While each silly pun makes my day feel complete.

I float on a cloud made of cotton candy,
Contemplating squids—yes, I know it's quite dandy.
With marshmallow musings, my heart takes a flight,
As I chuckle at shadows, they dance in the light.

In this land of reflection, my giggles take wing,
Like dolphins in uniforms, they all start to sing.
With mirth woven tightly, I bask in the sun,
For laughter's the treasure, and joy is the fun.

So come join the party, where thoughts intertwine,
With a buffet of chuckles and whirls all divine.
As I prance through the nonsense, my heart takes a bow,
In a ceiling of humor, I wonder 'What now?'

Threads of Yearning

I pull on the strands of my fanciful mind,
A tapestry woven with dreams so unkind.
A sock puppet whispers, 'Let's dance to the beat!'
While juggling my thoughts, I balance on feet.

With yarn made of stories, of joy and of fun,
Each thread that I grab leads to what's just begun.
My heart beats in mischief, it tickles my soul,
As I tumble through raindrops, they giggle and roll.

In the fabric of pondering, what do I seek?
A patch made of laughter, a stitch from the cheek.
I yearn for the whimsy, the comic delight,
As threads weave together, sparking thoughts bright.

So here's to the chaos, the wild and the weird,
In the quilt of my brain, so many have cheered.
Each thread tells a story, of joy to unfurl,
In this sitcom of thinking, let's all spin and twirl!

Veils of Unspoken Desires

In the garden of my mind, I grow,
A tangle of wishes, all in a row.
They peek out, giggle, and then hide,
Like socks in the dryer, nowhere to bide.

Whispers of pudding and chocolate cake,
Linger like secrets, a sweet little mistake.
I chase them with laughter, a fork in my hand,
To devour the dreams that I did not plan.

A cat with a monocle sits by my side,
He nods knowingly with much feline pride.
He counts all my hopes like counting his fish,
"Just tap a few more, they're all in the dish!"

Yet tangled in giggles, they flutter and flee,
Like butterflies soaring, so wild and so free.
I wonder if one day they'll come back to stay,
Or just pop like a bubble, and float far away.

The Interlace of Time's Remembrance

Tick-tock, the clock's a funny chap,
Wearing a hat, and taking a nap.
He yawns at the seconds, gives minutes a wink,
While I trip on the past, and spill all my ink.

Memories are noodles, they twist and they swirl,
Like pasta gone rogue, in an amusement whirl.
I sauce them with laughter and sprinkle with glee,
Then serve them to friends who all giggle with me.

Old photos are treasures that wear silly hats,
With mustaches and poses of all of my cats.
We dance on the weekends, we wheel and we spin,
With the ghosts of yesteryear joining in the din.

As time does its tango, I join in the fun,
A pirouette here, and I'm back to square one.
With moments entangled, I laugh at the fuss,
For every tick-tock is a playful plus.

Wreaths of Imagination

In the orchard of dreams, ideas take flight,
They swing on the branches, in colorful sight.
Some wear polka dots, others wear stripes,
While squirrels debate if they're ripe for the hype.

A flower once tried to gossip with bees,
But buzzed too much, and fell down with a wheeze.
It rolled in the dirt, turned purple and green,
Then laughed at itself; "I'm the best kind of queen!"

Paint splashes everywhere, a vibrant delight,
As crayons conspire to create a grand fight.
Counting to ten, then forgetting the score,
Like children in play, always asking for more.

So here in this world where whimsy rules bold,
I gather my wreaths of stories untold.
With ribbons and laughter, I toss them on high,
While the sun takes a bow, and echoes a sigh.

The Sway of Silent Reverie

On a breeze of daydreams, I sail with delight,
A ship made of giggles, I soar through the night.
My compass is wobbly, but who needs a map?
I'll fish for some stars, while I'm caught in the flap.

Whispers of nonsense drift softly around,
Like kittens who plot to be kings of the ground.
They tumble with charm, inventing new laws,
As I chuckle along, with a stretch and a yawn.

The clouds do the cha-cha and molds of the sun,
Daffodils dance when the day is done.
And right through my dreams, the absurdly profound,
A parade of my thoughts dances round and round.

So let's twirl with the shadows, and waltz with the light,
In the quiet of wonder, we'll spin with delight.
For in this grand reverie, laughter's the key,
Unlocking the joy of just being free.

www.ingramcontent.com/pod-product-compliance
Lightning Source LLC
Chambersburg PA
CBHW072134070526
44585CB00016B/1672